My mom's seance
candle holder

<u>Witch's Grimoire/Book of Shadows</u>- Is a textbook of magickal, it usually includes instructions on how to create and use magickal objects, how to perform magickal spells, make charms, divination and invoke spirits, Gods and Goddess's to help as well as a witches personal insight, spells and practice of witchcraft.

As I started on my personal journey of discovery with my (Soul-Sister) many years ago I felt pulled into this direction with memories from my childhood that I felt I needed to further understand. My mom passed away when I was 28 years old and I foretold of her pending death in a card reading I done for myself, I went to her and we discussed the interpretation. I really think she knew then that I seemed to have her abilities also and that she knew that it was her that the cards were warning of. She died

within a couple weeks of this. I have clear memories of standing at a

table as a child while my mom and her (friends) conducted a séance.

I can clearly see the kerosene lantern in the center of the table and

they were all holding hands and following my mom's instruction.

What I remember the most is the feeling I had watching, it was a

little bit of fear but mostly a vail of mystery and intrigue to me. We

had a giant cauldron in our back yard which was just there and I

didn't even think about it again until I began my witch studies all

those years later. As I started looking into the witch's path I could

look back at my childhood and see the signs that my mom was a witch everywhere in a lot of different ways. Witches bells hung by

our front door, her athame hung across from it also.

She had shelf upon shelf of books on all forms of divination. She had

talismans, gri-gris bags so many things all pointing to the witch's

path being one I believe she followed. I cherish the memories and feel

a deeper connection to her in my own witch practice. My sister and I

spent hours poring over books about everything witch, Wicca,

related. We started with the Gods/Goddesses then the elements of

earth, air, fire and water then moved on to studying the moon

phases. We learned about candle color meaning, incense, herbs,

athames, amulets, and various witches' tools. We learned how to cast a circle of protection for spell work, spell construction, incantations and crystals. We filled page after page of notebooks and binders with notes and computer printouts. Anything and everything we could find we read both in books as well as on the internet. I have included photos from some of my Grimoire's over the course of my personal years of study and spell work in this book.

Today we are both practicing witches. She has followed her path in a different direction than I; it is the witch after all that determines the purpose. Magic is neither dark nor white; it is the energy of nature molded by those who wield it. We still get together for Sewing (Voodoo Doll) magick and other rituals however mostly I practice alone. She started a Facebook page several years ago and we both contribute to it sharing our vast knowledge we have accumulated

over a course of more than 30+ years of practice in witchcraft. I am

an artist and have for many years struggled with putting myself

into my artwork. Suddenly I started having dreams about these

divination pieces and so I started to put them on paper and I shared

them with my sister and niece (also a practicing witch) to see what

they thought. I really expected the dreams and ideas would stop

after I did the first one but then they didn't and I started really

having a lot of fun with these pieces and so after the first couple I

decided to put them in this grimoire workbook. I have included some

photos taken of some of my personal grimoires which depict some

drawings and information which I have gathered over the course of my practice from many different resources and some of them are my own. It is my wish that you use this book as a guide to starting or continuing your practice of witchcraft. As Witches I think given our dark history it's important that we all hold each other up and support each other so that we never endure what our ancestors had to go through for the sake of their journey into witchcraft. The world is starting to accept our craft as the spiritual path that it is and it is my hope that someday witchcraft can be counted as an important spiritual entity in the world and may be given the same protection and respect from those who wish to harm that which they do not understand, as other spiritual paths.

<u>Book of Shadows Blessing-</u>

"You are my book of shadows, you are my way. Inside is my soul, each page a step further toward reaching my goal. So I ask the Goddess Hecate to protect every single page. Unto and after another book and unto and after this day and age; It is my will, so mote it be!" "This sacred space is where I may find myself again and again." A quote from Joseph Campbell

Personal Witch story

Gods/Goddess –

The **Horned god** represents the male part, consort of the female Triple goddess of the Moon or other Mother goddess. He is associated with nature, wilderness, sexuality, hunting, and the life cycle.

Hecate (Female Goddess) was the goddess of magick, witchcraft, the night, moon, ghosts and necromancy she was the only child of the Titans, Persis and Asteria from whom she received her power over heaven, earth, and sea. Perses was a Titan god in Greek mythology, son of the Titans Crius and Eurybia. He represented destruction and peace. He was married to the Titan goddess Asteria

* Necromancy is the practice of communicating with the dead, especially in order to predict the future which includes alchemy, necromancy, and other magical practices.

There are many Gods and Goddesses that are called upon in the practice of witchcraft and magick spell work which are each known for a different attribute. I suggest you research them as part of your practice of the craft before you call on them as some are not to be used lightly. All must be respected and thanked for their help.

<u>**Witches follow the moon when creating their spells;**</u> here are the phases which correspond to the 3 aspects of the Mother Goddess: Maiden, Mother, and Crone.

*<u>Triple Goddess</u> is viewed as a trinity of three distinct aspects or figures united in one being.

<u>**New Moon Magic:**</u> **(<u>Maiden</u>)** Attract new energies, a good time to

begin a new venture or project, plant the seed of your ideas; push

your energy toward renewal. This moon phase is all about

beginnings, so create spells for a new start.

____

____

____

____

____

____

<u>**Full Moon Magic; (Mother)**</u> Protection, Wisdom & Cleansing

flushing out and cultivating desire, an increase or gain to attract or

enhance the positive.

<u>**Waning Moon Magic: (Crone)**</u> light decreasing rid you of unwanted influence and decrease negative qualities or situations.

<u>**Incantation~**</u> "Moon of finest silver wane, take with you bad luck and bane, as you fade into the night, bring new hope back into sight as I will it, so mote it be."

____

____

____

____

____

____

When the moon is in your own sun sign it's your personal best time for your magick to work. Spells work on multiple levels essentially which is a form of prayer/manifestation. Each person has a different vibrational response so approach a spell with purpose, quiet focus and clarity. When one spell doesn't work you may try another but keep in mind that some spells take longer to manifest then others so don't panic have patients waiting for results. Always Thank the Gods and Goddess's and end spells with "it is my will, So Mote it be!"

*Some witch's follow the law of three I however do not so if you wish to, then do your research first.

<u>**The 4 Elements of magick are Earth, Air, Fire and Water:**</u>

<u>**Earth**</u>- witches stones/crystals, fertility, purification, the home and money

<u>**Air**</u>- Incense, intellect, writing, study, astral travel, and music

<u>**Fire**</u>- candle/cauldron, protection, career, legal matters, banishing, cleansing, courage and strength

<u>**Water**</u>- chalice/cauldron, childbirth, cleansing, psychic awareness and rebirth

<u>**Incantation:**</u> "I call upon the powers that be, to bring what I want straight to me. By fire, air, earth and sea, it is my will, so mote it be!"

<u>Tools of the Craft-</u>

Witch's use many objects in their magic. Candles, stones and crystals essential oils, talismans, amulets, the list is long and I recommend that you study them all and then decide which of these elements you think work best for you. One thing I do know is that not all magick is the same and like I said earlier, each person brings their own energy essence into magick. I have used many of the tools available to a witch throughout my many years of practice. The thing about being a witch is that for most of us it's a very personal journey. I think we all find our paths lead us to a place where we are comfortable enough and have learned enough that we can just hone our magick to a very strong power and need fewer rituals to achieve what we want, at least that is how it is for me.

Spell construction:

1. Write down your magickal goal/intent

2. Write down moon phase (if following) date, time and any notes you think will help you with your incantation/manifestation of your spell.

3. Determine if you need a full circle casting (research how to cast a circle) or a simple spell work

4. Write down ingredients you will need for your spell such as candles, incense, stones/crystals, wand and if using divination tools like tarot cards, tea leaves, runes, symbols, crystal ball, scrying etc.,

5. Record spells in your grimoire (this guide grimoire/book of shadows)

<u>Spell Construction</u>

____

____

____

____

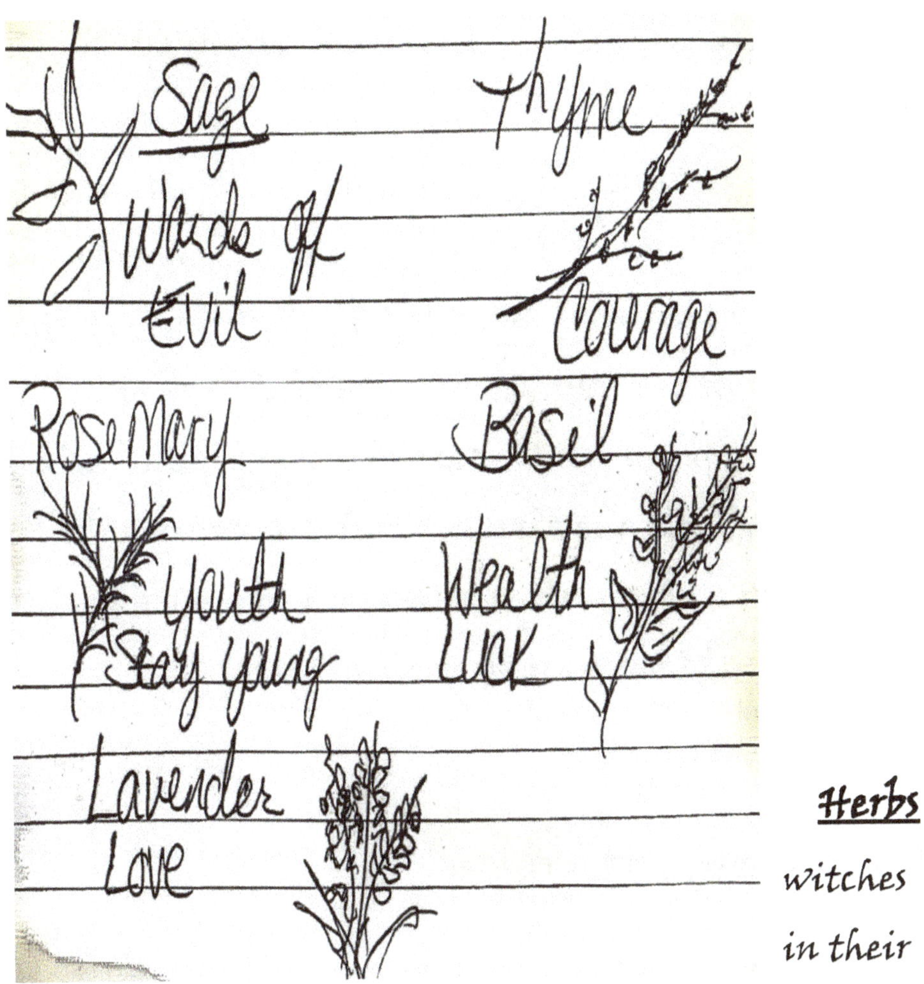

witches

in their

Witches
use herbs

Most. There are literally hundreds+ of different herbs available for use in spell work and there are literally thousands + of information and resources available to you for research on which herbs to use for which type spell you are working. Some witch's prefer to cultivate their own garden while others buy theirs from the literally hundreds + sources available to purchase them. My rule of thumb is don't get caught up in the how as much as in the purpose, meaning it's not as important how you get/purchase your herbs as much as knowing what each one is used for and why you use it in your practice/spell work. I buy mine from the store or even a specialty shop specific for witches and some my Sister gives me; I have some from the grocery store so really they are available almost everywhere. Here is a simple list of grocery store alternatives you probably already have in your own pantry right now and what they represent along with a list of my most used herbs and their symbolism and uses. Like I said there is a huge amount you have available so I recommend you research and find what works best for your spiritual practice.

<u>Black tea</u>/ <u>Mug wort</u>- Courage

<u>Pecan/Devil's Shoestring</u>- employment

<u>Allspice</u>- Protection and Luck

<u>Blackberry/ Trillium</u> - Money

Barley/ Bloodroot- Protection

Salt/Benzoin- Purification

Ginger/ Rowan- Safe Travels, Success

Celery seed- Increases physical and mental powers

Mustard seed- Protection and to Increase mental powers and faith

Basil- Is a go to herb for me, I literally use it in everything both for recipes and spell work. It is considered to be the most sacred herb and is kept in the home to protect against evil, and believed to have wonderful healing powers (I use it to make a tea for bladder/kidney infections it is said to have antibacterial properties) It is used in spell work for banishing and protection, prosperity and luck, success and business, clarity and courage.

Mint- Another go to herb for me is mint, a calming and soothing herb I use this herb and oil both in so many ways for healing or as a tea for stomach and digestion problems, great for soaking tired achy feet and spell work. It is a symbol of protection so I use it in all protection spells and as an aid for protecting both my person (in a witches pouch) and my home.

Witchy Tip: Wash down your front door with warm water and mint essential oil to refresh the vibrations and bring in luck, wealth and abundance, if you don't have the oil you can use tea as an alternative.

Sage- Symbolizes protection, drives out evil and wards off bad luck. Sage is used in many rituals and spell work, sage is often burned to rid people and spaces of negative energy and spirits; it also generates wisdom, clarity and promotes healing. I started many years ago putting sage and other herbs in my scents pot burner along with the wax melts.

<u>**Incantation:**</u> *A Smudging incantation & Prayer for self-protection*

"I seek protection and sound my alarm, may my body, mind and spirit be safe from harm; I am surrounded by positive energy to shield and protect me from all harm; I am strong and block negative energy and all that is wrong. Negative energy you may not stay, I release you be on your way; from here on out I banish thee, these are my words, so mote it be."

<u>**Rosemary-**</u> Youth, a symbol of happiness, purity, friendship, loyalty and love, banishing and protection. It is also considered the herb of remembrance and some people use it to honor the dead. It is said to have antiseptic, antioxidant and anti-inflammatory properties for healing and it helps to improve digestion and enhance memory.

<u>**Thyme:**</u> Courage, like sage thyme can be burned to banish evil and purify the home. It is said to bring clarity and is used to enhance psychic abilities.

Lavender- Love, purity, serenity, devotion and calmness also relaxation, peace, protection, clarity and wishes; this is a great herb used as a tea or tincture for healing both physically and spiritually. Lavender can be burned to promote calmness and remove negative energy.

Chamomile- Purification and protection it also has a very calming effect and can be used to promote sleep and help with meditation and relaxation; this herb also brings luck and has healing properties. I use it as a tea when I have a cold or flu to help promote healing.

Bay Leaves- Removes negative energy and protection

Witchy tip: Write symbols of protection on bay leaves and burn them; (Also write them on tea bags (match variety to its magickal properties and carry them with you, put in your car for safe travels; I even put them in my window sills to protect my home.)

<u>**Rose Petals-**</u> Symbolizes love and luck

<u>**Mugwort-**</u> Considered the universal herb for protection and prophecy throughout the ancient world. Roman soldiers placed mugwort inside their sandals for endurance in long marches. Also known as the visionary herb, Native Americans used mugwort as a "smudge" to purify the spiritual and physical environment. Today witches uses mugwort for spell work and to increase psychic powers.

As I have said there are literally thousand+ herbs used in the practice of witchcraft so I recommend you research them all as I have and then use what works best for you. I know some say that you have to do everything a certain way and use exact ingredients and incantations etc. I think if that's what you need to do for your personal practice of witchcraft then so be it. I however use what I know works for me; however, as I have said Research, research, research is how I came to that conclusion and why I strongly recommend you do the same.

<u>Herbs</u>

Stones & Crystals

<u>Clear Quartz</u>-Balance, master healer this is my go to crystal because it has an absorbing quality and is great for absorbing negative energy. I hold one in each hand as I meditate and in vision stress and negative energy leaving my body and flowing into the crystal. Afterward they will appear to have a darker color from absorbing the negativity so I am sure to recharge and cleanse them in salt or moonlight.

<u>Rose Quartz</u>-Love, balance, heals and rejuvenates emotions

<u>Lepidolite</u> - Courage, Calms the heart and mind, eases stress and depression it is said to promote deep emotional healing

<u>Citrine</u>- Raises self-esteem, attracts joy and grounds negative energy

<u>Amethyst</u>-A violet variety of quartz, it is the premiere spiritual stone for psychic awareness; success, purification and spiritual protection, barrier against psychic attack

*See photo below of my artwork, Amethyst

<u>Black Onyx-</u> A powerful stone for protection it absorbs negative energy and is said to guard from the evil eye.

and Love energy, for life Wealth money, prosperity are literally different crystals the practice of

power and a zest
<u>Ruby-</u> Courage success and
<u>Emerald & Jade-</u> hundreds of and stones used in ~~like herbs there~~

34

witchcraft so you may want to research some more. This is just a few of the ones I use in my personal practice but again the thing about witchcraft is that it is a very personal practice and we each need to determine what works for us.

Crystals & Stones

This is a page from one of my Grimoires

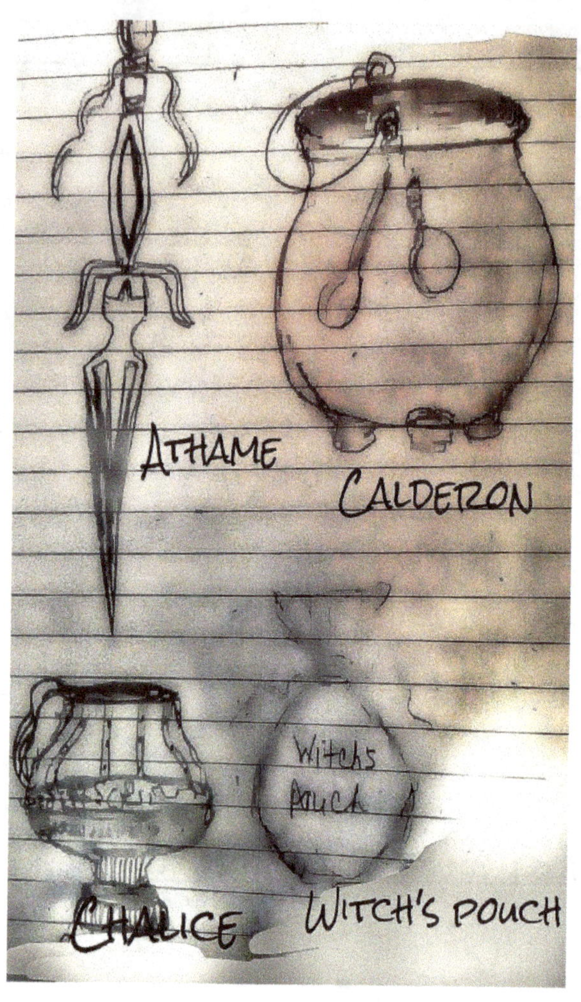

ATHAME
CALDERON
Witchs pouch
CHALICE
WITCH'S POUCH

The tools of witchcraft are something all witches use and have on

their (alters) they are used for spell craft and to honor the

Gods/Goddess in rituals. They are something I have over the years

come to realize are very personal to each witch and a large part of

their individual practice.

Candles, Incense & Salt

These items are all used in witchcraft for spell work for
cleansing/purification and on witches alter, to represent the
elements fire, Air, and water. (Research candle magick & color meanings;
white is a universal color and can be used in any type of spell work.)

Amulet/Talisman

An amulet also called a good luck charm by some is believed to have

the power to ward off bad luck, negative energy and spirits they are a small object that is typically worn/carried on your person. It can

be jewelry, small stones; anything really that has meaning for an

individual or that a person gives power to. A talisman on the other

hand is said to give power to the individual wearing it.

Athame

  An athame or ceremonial blade/knife is a tool used by many

witches who practice witchcraft as a cutting tool both ritualistic

and physically for cutting herbs often used in spells and rituals. It is

a very powerful tool and can be used to protect against unwanted

spirits.

Cauldron

A cauldron is a cast iron pot used for thousands of years under an open outdoor flame for rituals and spell work. While I don't have or use a cauldron I have clear memories of us having one in our backyard where I grew up however I never saw my Mom use ours for a specific purpose, I do think she probably did at some point in her life as a practice of witchcraft.

Chalice

A cup or goblet typically used for drinking water, wine, herbal teas or symbolically in the practice of a ritual or spell.

Witches Pouch

used to carry witches tools of witchcraft it is a pouch made from leather, hide or some form of material. Witches use them to carry herbs, crystals, runes, hag stones and other small bits used for the practice of their magic.

Runes/Hag Stones:

This is a photo taken from one of my Grimoires depicting the symbols carved into stone or wood that is used as a form of divination in witchcraft. If you wish to try them make sure to research before you either make or buy some.

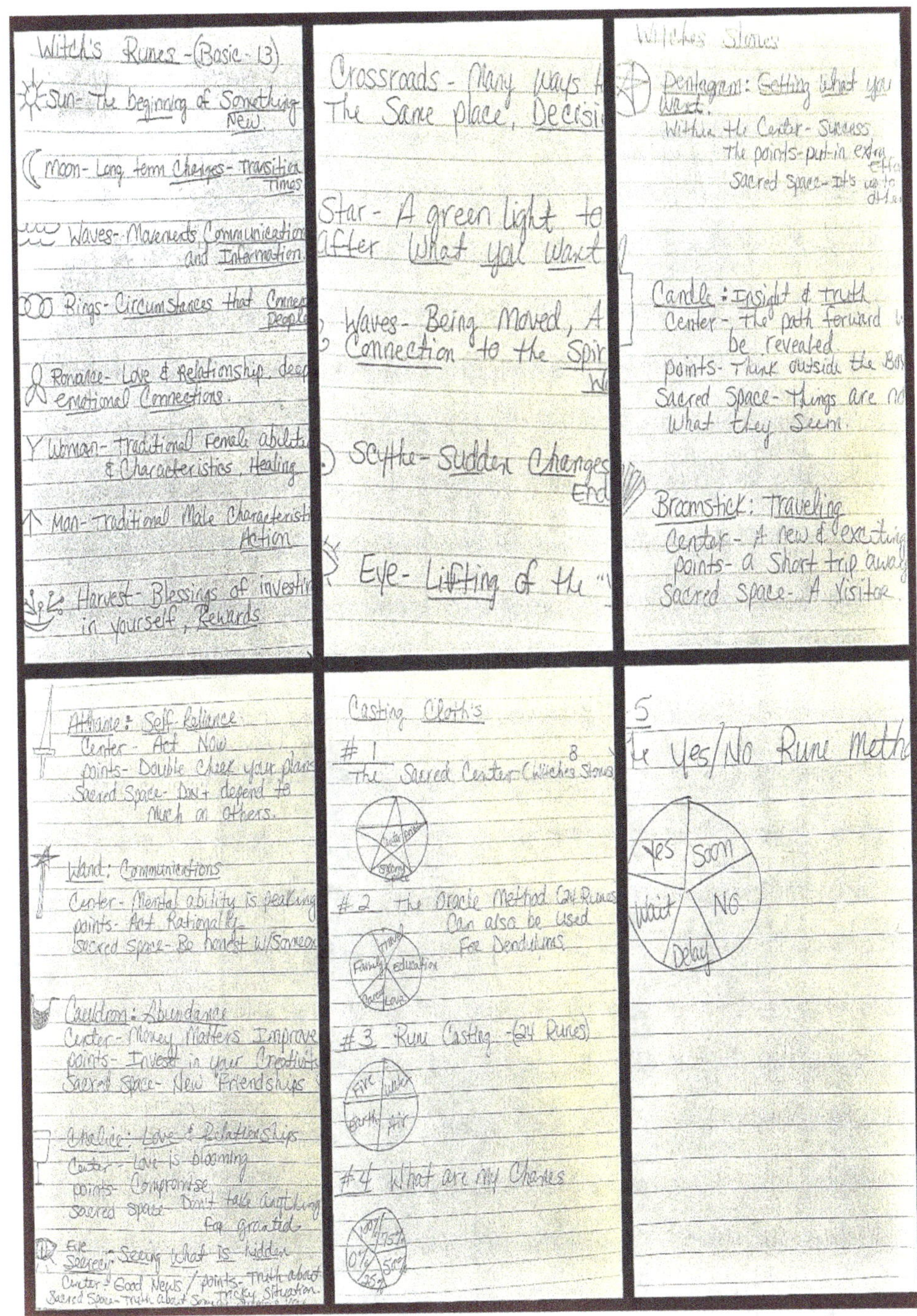

Witch's Runes - (Basic - 13)

☼ Sun - The beginning of Something New

☽ Moon - Long term Changes - Transition Times

〜 Waves - Movements, Communication and Information.

⚬⚬⚬ Rings - Circumstances that Connect People

♀ Romance - Love & Relationship, deep emotional Connections.

Y Woman - Traditional Female abilities & Characteristics, Healing.

↑ Man - Traditional Male Characteristics Action

Harvest - Blessings of investing in yourself, Rewards

Crossroads - Many Ways to The Same place, Decision

Star - A green light to After What you Want

Waves - Being Moved, A Connection to the Spirit World

Scythe - Sudden Changes End

Eye - Lifting of the "Veil"

Witches Stones

⊕ Pentagram: Getting what you Want.
Within the Center - Success
The points - put in extra Effort
Sacred Space - It's up to Others

Candle : Insight & truth
Center - The path forward will be revealed
points - Think outside the Box
Sacred Space - Things are not What they Seem.

Broomstick: Traveling
Center - A new & exciting
points - a Short trip away
Sacred Space - A Visitor.

Athame : Self-Reliance
Center - Act Now
points - Double Check your plans
Sacred Space - Don't depend to Much on Others.

Wand: Communications
Center - Mental ability is peaking
points - Act Rationally
Sacred Space - Be honest w/Someone

Cauldron: Abundance
Center - Money Matters Improve
points - Invest in your Creativity
Sacred Space - New Friendships

Chalice : Love & Relationships
Center - Love is blooming
points - Compromise
Sacred Space - Don't take anything for granted.

Eye
Secrecy : Seeing what is hidden
Center - Good News / points - Truth about Tricky situation.
Sacred Space - Truth about Something

Casting Cloth's

#1 The Sacred Center - (Witches Stones)

#2 The Oracle Method (24 Runes)
Can also be Used For Pendulums

#3 Rune Casting - (24 Runes)

#4 What are my Chances

5

#5 Yes/No Rune Method

<u>**Besom/Broom**</u> The picture on the right is of my besom which I have had for many years it was made for me as a gift. They are used by witches to sweep away unwanted spirits and energy; if kept by the front door it is said to ward off unwanted visitors.

<u>**Witch Bells**</u>-The picture on the left is of my witch bells used to call spirits, evoke good energy and they may be hung on a door knob to protect the home.

44

<u>Witches Alter~</u>

 A Witches altar is a special structure or place used for spell work and rituals most practitioners of witchcraft have at least one; where they keep tools and other items for the purpose of calling on the God and Goddess, casting spells, and/or saying chants and incantations.

<u>List the tools used for your practice of witchcraft</u>

____

____

<u>Cleansing & Charging</u>

One of the most important things to remember about all of your tools

of witchcraft is that whether they are found, purchased used, given

to you as a gift or brand new they all must be cleansed of old energy

and charged with new/your energy before use and/or before using in

spell work or rituals. This should be done for all tools crystals,

athames, wands, herbs, amulets etc. There are a lot of ways to do this

but, I will just name a few and you can research other methods for

yourself.

The best ways to cleanse/charge is to use the elements sun/moon

energy, water, salt, fire, incense or a candle which of these you use will depend on what the item is to be cleansed. Do research if you are

unsure but for example some crystals cannot be cleansed with water

or you wouldn't throw your besom/broom into a fire directly but may

pass it through the smoke. I typically use salt, sun/moon energy the

most. I like to hold each item in my hand (if possible) for a few

minutes so that it can absorb my magical energy especially if it's a

tool I will use often such as an athame, amulet, and besom etc. you

definitely need to be sure everything is charged before any magick

spell work; always cleanse after you finish.

There are options which as I said I have not discussed here but there is

plenty of books and internet websites that you can research on your

own.

Symbols

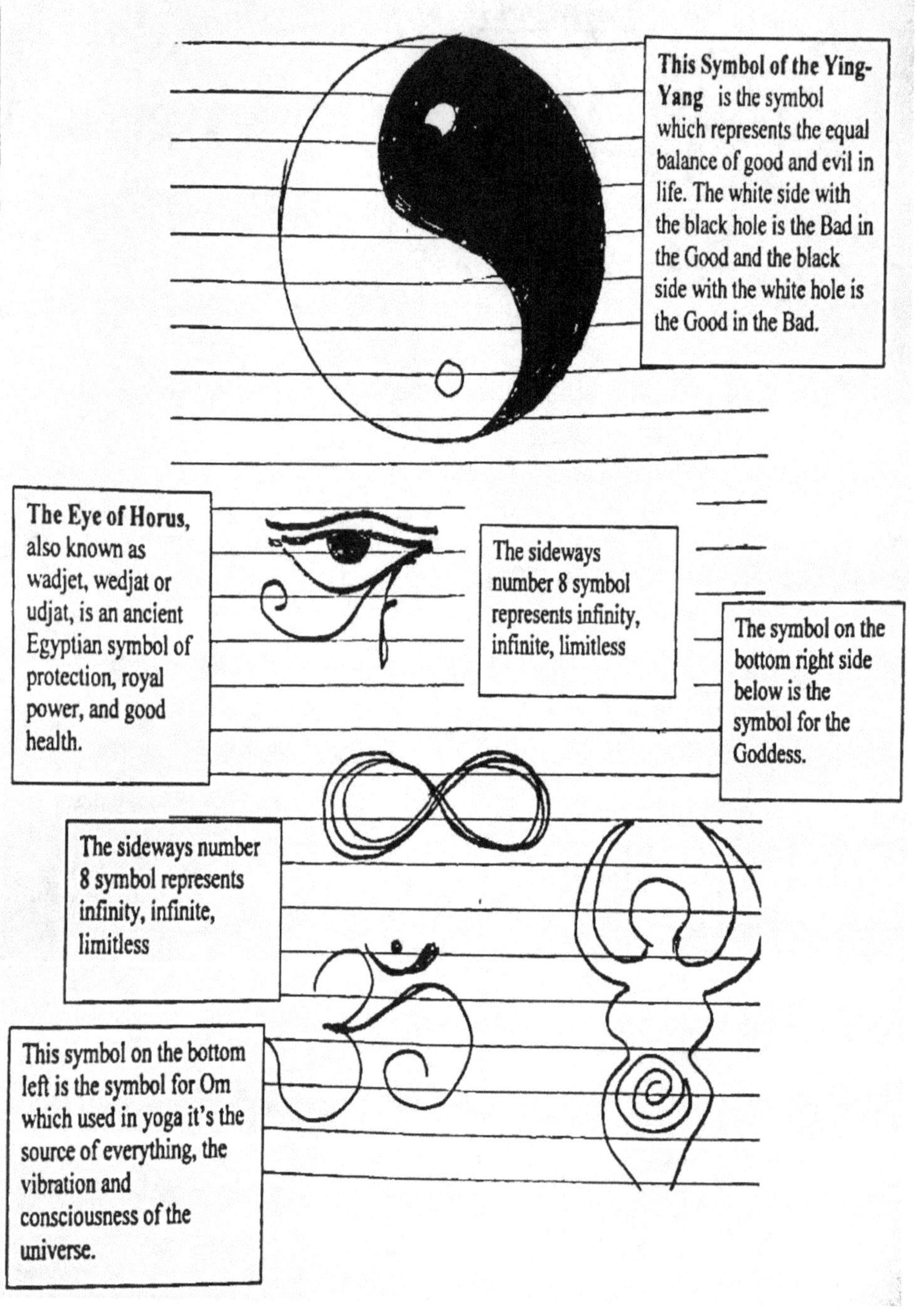

This Symbol of the Ying-Yang is the symbol which represents the equal balance of good and evil in life. The white side with the black hole is the Bad in the Good and the black side with the white hole is the Good in the Bad.

The Eye of Horus, also known as wadjet, wedjat or udjat, is an ancient Egyptian symbol of protection, royal power, and good health.

The sideways number 8 symbol represents infinity, infinite, limitless

The symbol on the bottom right side below is the symbol for the Goddess.

The sideways number 8 symbol represents infinity, infinite, limitless

This symbol on the bottom left is the symbol for Om which used in yoga it's the source of everything, the vibration and consciousness of the universe.

There are many different symbols used in the practice of witchcraft they are seen in grimoires, amulets, talismans, spells and many forms of divination. There are also different things to which they represent; there are symbols for prosperity, health, safe travel, love, luck and many more; they are used for protection from the evil eye/bad spirits and those who wish to harm. In divination the symbols are interpreted in different ways depending on how they are presented and which form of divination you are using. The most popular and also misunderstood symbol used in witchcraft is the Pentagram which is a 5 pointed star and the pentacle which is a 5 pointed star inside a circle. The word pentacle originally meant any symbol that protects against evil spirits; there are a lot of these types of symbols but only a few of which include a pentagram. Both mean

the same thing and are used as a symbol of protection.

Triple Goddess

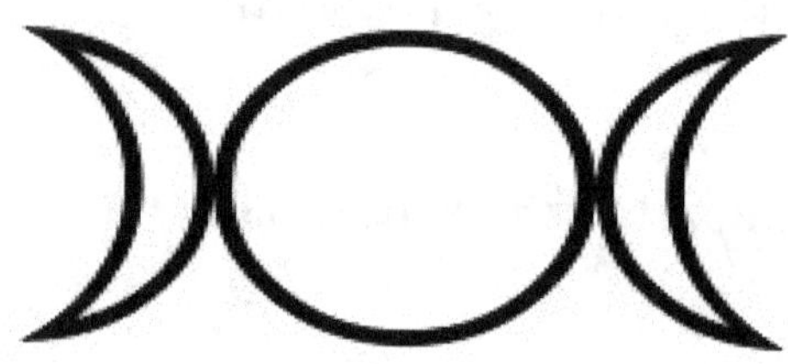

Triple Goddess

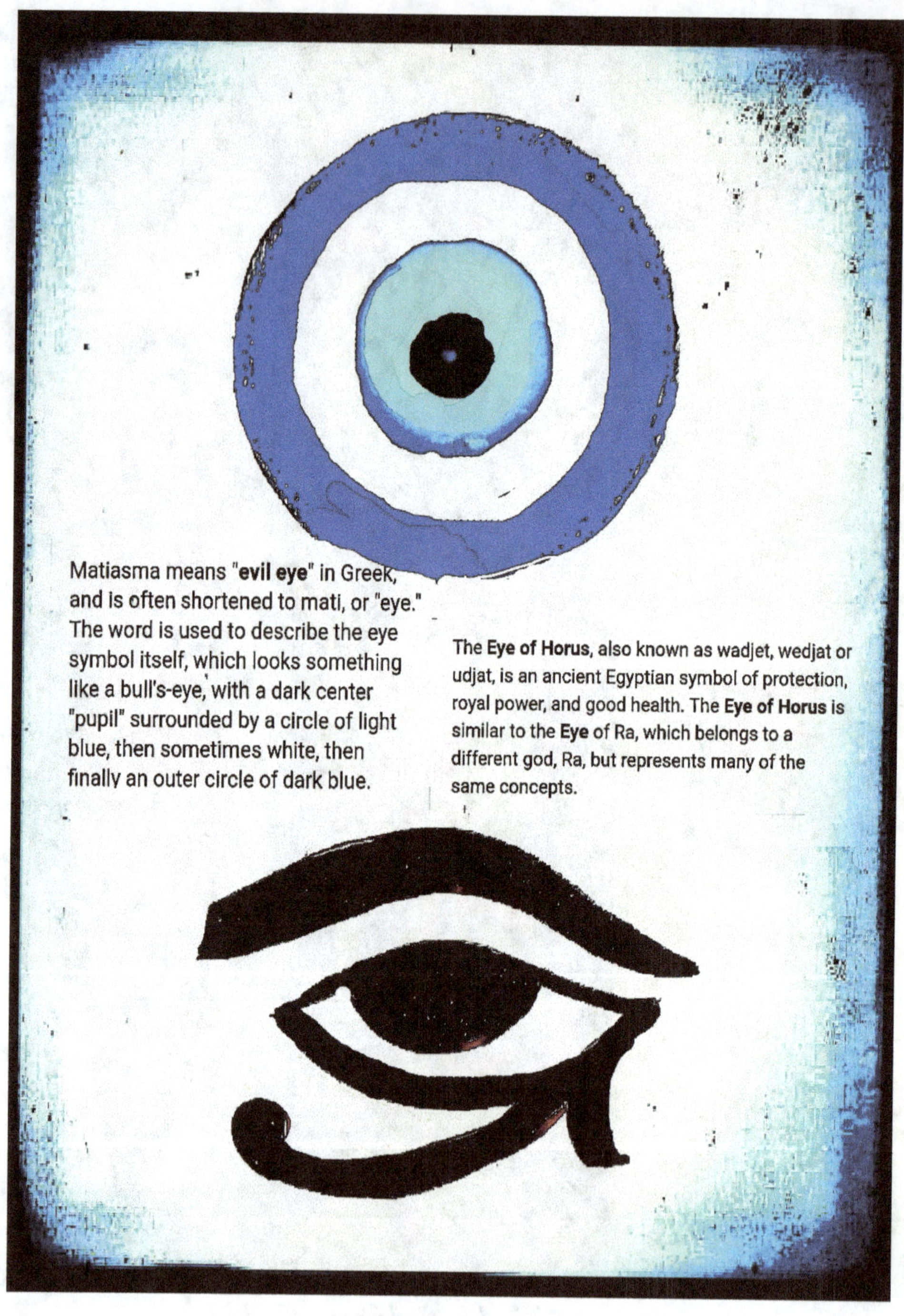

Matiasma means "**evil eye**" in Greek, and is often shortened to mati, or "eye." The word is used to describe the eye symbol itself, which looks something like a bull's-eye, with a dark center "pupil" surrounded by a circle of light blue, then sometimes white, then finally an outer circle of dark blue.

The **Eye of Horus**, also known as wadjet, wedjat or udjat, is an ancient Egyptian symbol of protection, royal power, and good health. The **Eye of Horus** is similar to the **Eye** of Ra, which belongs to a different god, Ra, but represents many of the same concepts.

Evil Eye & Eye of Horace

Hamsa is a talismanic symbol that people believed to protect them from harm against the evil forces. The **Hamsa** Hand or Hand of Fatima is an ancient Middle Eastern talisman. In all religions it is a protective symbol. ... The amulet consists of five spread fingers, often with an eye on the hand.

Hamsa Hand

Hamsa Hand

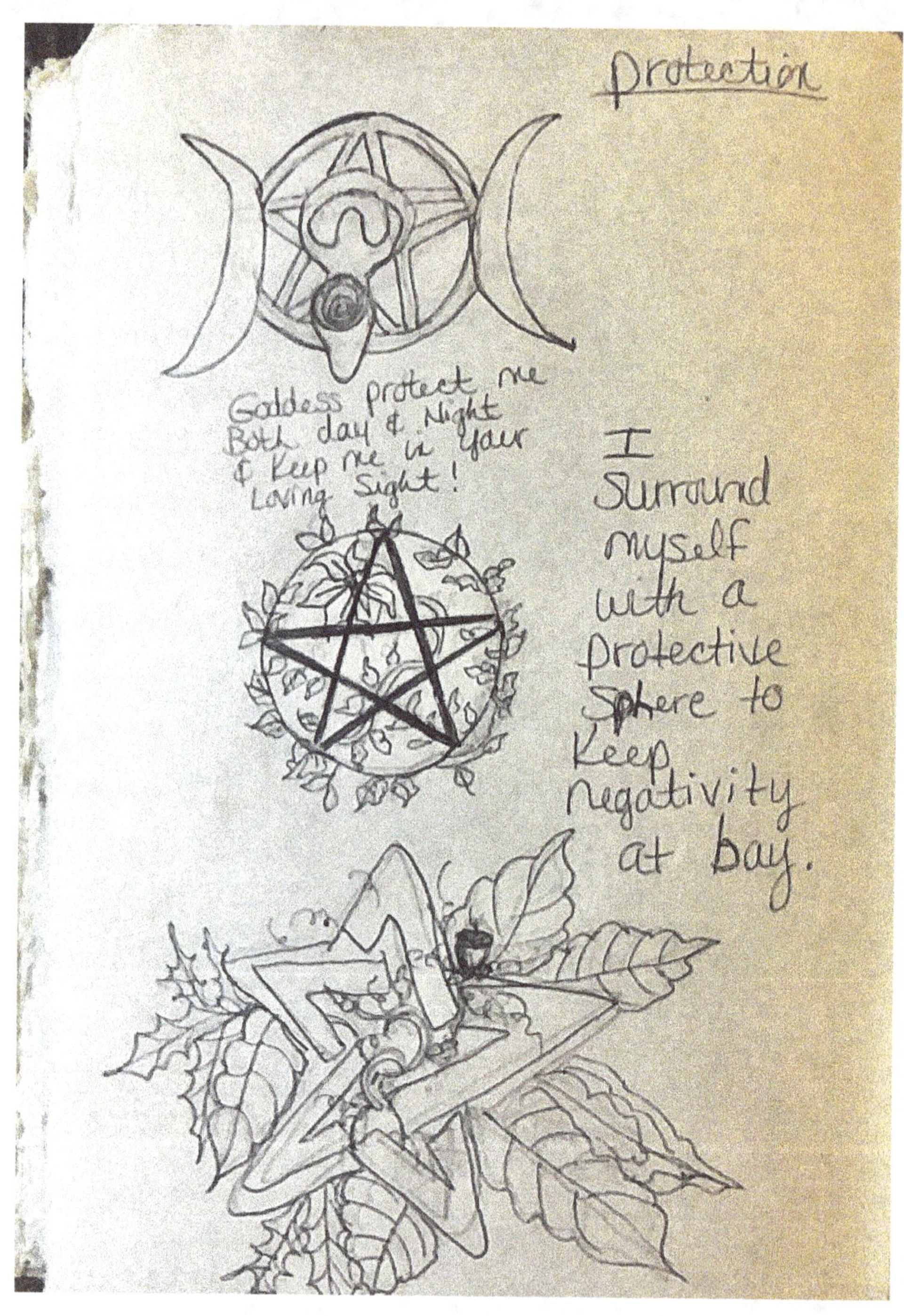

Pages from one of my Grimoires

May there always be work
for your hands to do,
May your purse always hold a
Coin or Two, May the Sun
always Shine upon your
window pane, May a
Rainbow be certain to follow
each rain, May the hand
of a friend always be near
to you, May Goddess fill
your heart with Gladness
to Cheer you!

Symbol Drawings

Symbol Meanings

____

____

____

Divination

Divination Is derived from the Latin divinare, meaning to foresee, to foretell, to predict, or to prophesy; to be inspired by a god is the attempt to gain insight into a question or situation by way of a process or ritual; the practice of seeking knowledge of the future or the unknown by supernatural means, The Celtic art of divination which represents fortune telling; divining foretelling the future forecasting the future.

Tarot/fortune telling Cards

Cartomancy is fortune-telling or divination using a deck of cards. In English-speaking countries, the most common form of cartomancy is generally tarot card reading. There are all different types of cards available. I suggest you research them prior to buying any and then get the ones that you feel comfortable with, let the cards pick you. I use regular playing cards and I have several different types of Tarot cards also; remember to charge them with your magical energy prior to your first use.

Tarot

They are commonly **used to** measure potential outcomes and evaluate influences surrounding a person, an event, or both. The technical term for **tarot** reading is taromancy (divination through the use of **tarot** cards), which is a subsection of cartomancy (divination through cards in general).

tarot card designs

<u>Horoscope</u>

Each of the 12 sections of a horoscope is called zodiac signs. A horoscope is the position of the planets and house cusps, and Moon's nodes at the moment a person is born. A horoscope is also often called a birth chart by astrologers. (Research before making a birth chart)

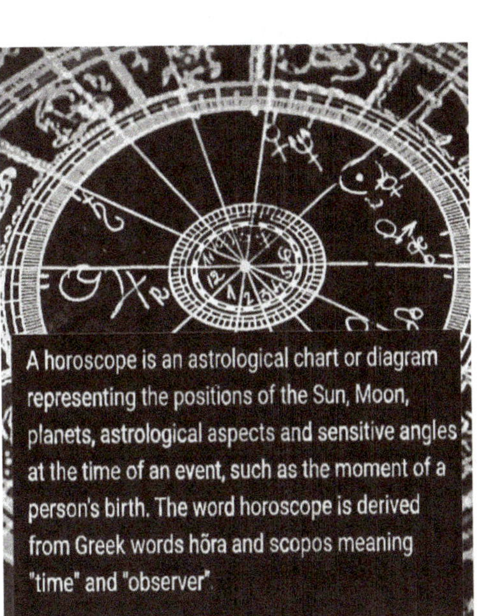

<u>Crystal Ball</u>

A crystal ball, also known as an orbuculum or crystal sphere, is a crystal or glass ball and common fortune-telling object. The use of crystal balls to predict the future is viewed as pseudoscience.

Crystal balls have been used for at least four thousand years for divination. The art of gaining information for looking into **crystal** is called "scrying." Most people associate a gypsy **reading crystal ball** as a symbol of mystical power.

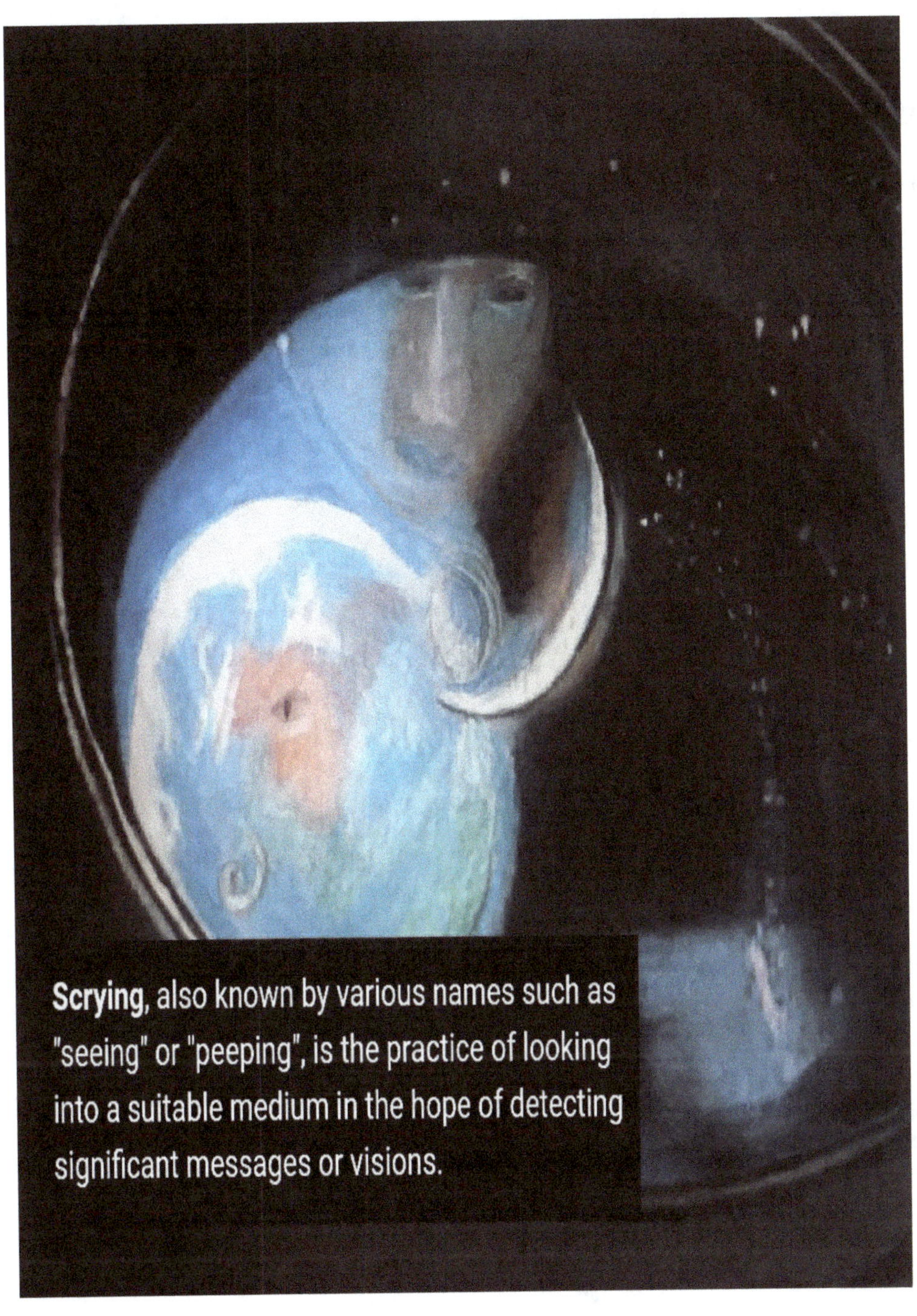

<u>Water Scrying</u>- (can also done using a mirror)

<u>**Palmistry**</u>

Palmistry or chiromancy is the claim of characterization and foretelling the future through the study of the palm, also known as chirology, or in popular culture as palm reading. (Research before reading, there are a lot of good books on the subject)

Palm reading
Palmestry
Heart line
Head line
Lifeline
1ST KNOT
1ST
2ND PHALANX
3RD
MOUNT OF VENUS
UPPER MARS
MOUNT OF MOON

Tasseography is a divination or fortune-telling method that interprets patterns in tea leaves after the tea is finished being consumed, many people believed that tea leaf reading originated in China. Today tea leaf reading is thought to have originated in Asia, the Middle East and Ancient Greece. Tea leaf reading began to grow in popularity during the 1800's as a means of telling one's fortune/future and was spread by nomadic gypsies throughout Europe. (Research tea leaf meanings)

<u>**Séance**</u>

French ... word

which ... means

sitting; in

witchcraft is a meeting centered on a medium who seeks to communicate with spirits of the dead. Because strong light is said to hinder communication, a séance usually takes place in darkness or subdued light. The artwork above shows a kerosene lantern which I remember is what my Mom used during a séance.

<u>**Pendulums**</u>

A Pendulum is used to promote healing through the process of dowsing which seeks out invisible energies. This connects people to a higher energy spiritually and can help locate any blocks in energy. They are also used as a form of divination in witchcraft by asking questions to receive guidance, awareness, and understanding.

A pendulum works by converting energy back and forth. The type of crystal used as a pendulum varies depending on what you are trying to do. You should use a clear quartz pendulum for clarity, Amethyst pendulums are best used for its strong spiritual connection, and if you are looking for a pendulum to help with love and matters of the heart, then one made from rose quartz should be used.

<u>**Numerology**</u>

Numerology is any belief in the divine or mystical relationship between a number and one or more coinciding events. It is also the study of the numerical value of the letters in words, names, and ideas. It is often associated with astrology and similar divinatory arts. Numerology is the study of numbers in your life; you can uncover information about the world and also each individual person by using numerology. In order to find your Life (soul) number, simply take your birthdate and reduce it down to its numerical value. For example, if you were born on November 15, 1989, you'd first identify the separate values of the day, month, and year. November is the 11th month, so its number is 11. Your day of birth is, 15 and the year of your birth is 1989. To determine what your life (soul) number is add your birth month and birth day $1+1+1+5 = 8$. Now add you're birth year as $1+9+8+9 = 27$ which would be reduced to $2+7 = 9$. So $8+9 = 17$ which would be further reduced to $1+7 = 8$ is your life (soul) number. <u>**(Soul) Number**</u> – Birth Month + Birth Day +

Birth Year (Reduced) =

____

____

Traditional Pagan Sabbats

<u>Yule- December 22nd</u> - Winter Solstice the Pagan celebration of Winter Solstice (also known as Yule) it is one of the oldest winter celebrations in the world.

<u>Imbolc- February 2nd</u> - Based on a Celtic tradition, Imbolc was meant to mark the halfway point between winter solstice and the spring equinox

<u>Ostara- March 22nd</u> - Ostara is a time of new fire; the light and dark are in perfect balance, but the light is growing and the sun is about to burst forth with new energy. Ostara is a season of fertility and growth.

<u>Beltane- May 1st</u>- Beltane or Beltain is the Gaelic May Day festival. It is held halfway between the spring equinox and the summer solstice.

<u>Midsummer Solstice- June 22nd</u>- Otherwise known as the festival of solstice, midsummer or Litha it is the longest day of the year. It occurs when the earth's geographical pole on either the northern or southern hemisphere becomes the most inclined towards the sun and officially marks the beginning of summer.

Lammas (Lughnasadh) - August 1st -

Lughnasadh, also called Lammas, falls roughly halfway between the summer solstice and autumn equinox. The early harvest and the threshing of grain have been celebrated for thousands of years.

Mabon - September 22nd -

A harvest festival it is the second of three which encourages pagans to "reap what they sow," both literally and figuratively. It is the time when night and day stand equal in duration; it is a time to express gratitude complete projects and honor a moment of balance.

Samhain (Sauin, Sawin) - October 31st

Is a Gaelic festival marking the end of the harvest season and the beginning of winter or the darker half of the year. Traditionally, it is celebrated from 31 October to 1 November, as the Celtic day began and ended at sunset. This is about halfway between the autumn equinox and the winter solstice. Today it is gaining popularity as a major celebration in the United States and is often referred to as Halloween or All Hallows Eve.

Esbats -

Traditional pagan full moon rituals

My final thoughts & wishes as you walk this path with me.

It is my hope that you can take this Grimoire (Book of Shadows) guide and use it to help you start or continue your own book/Grimoire. I really believe that I was meant to write this book as a further journey on my own personal path as a witch. I can see that I didn't really start my own journey into witchcraft until after my mom passed away. I couldn't explain the memories I had of her and all the things that were a part of my life growing up that I didn't even think about at the time. The memories and feelings that I still get to this day every time I remember our conversation when I shared my divination (Card Reading) about a death that would take place and we could only look at one another both knowing it was her that would die soon, I am reminded of a similar story she told me about the same thing happening to her as well. She also had a similar card in her reading which predicted an accidental death and my Dad was a truck driver at the time so when he went over the road a couple of days after that she worried sick about him. A few days after he returned she got a call that her Mother had passed away; when she got the final death certificate it read the she died from an accidental cerebral hemorrhage. It was a little later that she realized that she read it in her cards but that the accident referred to

in the interpretation wasn't a vehicle accident. The parallels I often
find with her life and practice of witchcraft are a comfort to me now
because they make me feel close to her in a way I think most people
can't understand. I believe we are still so connected that we share a
magical strength that sometime even frightens me to be honest. I just
know that my journey through witchcraft has been one of the most
personal things in my life that I have always held private and dear
to me. I haven't shared these events with more than 1 or 2 people who
know me because to me it's a connection to my Mom which I want to
keep to myself. I reflected on why I was so driven to write this book
and I really think she was there in my dreams guiding me all
through it. I know I am one of the lucky ones to be able to walk this
path into witchcraft and know with no doubt that it is my destiny.
I hope all witches can feel that as well and above all honor those
who have walked before us, as I honor my mother and her mother and
on and on.

A Blessing of Thanks

"I give you thanks for all you do, for obstacles and smooth roads to. For challenges that make me grow, and all the love and warmth you show, that you are looking after me, I Thank you Ancients. Blessed Be."

<u>Notes</u>

____

____

____

____

____

____

Most of the information used in this book was obtained over the course of 30+ years of study and while I cannot possibly name every single reference I will say that it includes many book and internet sources available to the public as well as my own understanding and insight.

9 798392 506897